Bills And Payments Organizer

This book belongs to:

....

....

IF FOUND CONTACT:

....

• Contents •

• Bonus Chapters •

• SUBSCRIPTIONS TRACKER •

SUBSCRIPTION	DUE ON	AMOUNT	FREQUENCY		AUTO RENEW	
			Monthly	Yearly	Yes	No
1.		$	○	○	○	○
2.		$	○	○	○	○
3.		$	○	○	○	○
4.		$	○	○	○	○
5.		$	○	○	○	○
6.		$	○	○	○	○
7.		$	○	○	○	○
8.		$	○	○	○	○
9.		$	○	○	○	○
10.		$	○	○	○	○
11.		$	○	○	○	○
12.		$	○	○	○	○
13.		$	○	○	○	○
14.		$	○	○	○	○
15.		$	○	○	○	○
16.		$	○	○	○	○
17.		$	○	○	○	○
18.		$	○	○	○	○
19.		$	○	○	○	○
20.		$	○	○	○	○
21.		$	○	○	○	○

• SUBSCRIPTIONS TRACKER •

SUBSCRIPTION	DUE ON	AMOUNT	FREQUENCY		AUTO RENEW	
			Monthly	Yearly	Yes	No
22.		$	○	○	○	○
23.		$	○	○	○	○
24.		$	○	○	○	○
25.		$	○	○	○	○
26.		$	○	○	○	○
27.		$	○	○	○	○
28.		$	○	○	○	○
29.		$	○	○	○	○
30.		$	○	○	○	○
31.		$	○	○	○	○
32.		$	○	○	○	○
33.		$	○	○	○	○
34.		$	○	○	○	○
35.		$	○	○	○	○
36.		$	○	○	○	○
37.		$	○	○	○	○
38.		$	○	○	○	○
39.		$	○	○	○	○
40.		$	○	○	○	○
41.		$	○	○	○	○
42.		$	○	○	○	○

• SUBSCRIPTIONS TRACKER •

SUBSCRIPTION	DUE ON	AMOUNT	FREQUENCY		AUTO RENEW	
			Monthly	Yearly	Yes	No
43.		$	○	○	○	○
44.		$	○	○	○	○
45.		$	○	○	○	○
46.		$	○	○	○	○
47.		$	○	○	○	○
48.		$	○	○	○	○
49.		$	○	○	○	○
50.		$	○	○	○	○
51.		$	○	○	○	○
52.		$	○	○	○	○
53.		$	○	○	○	○
54.		$	○	○	○	○
55.		$	○	○	○	○
56.		$	○	○	○	○
57.		$	○	○	○	○
58.		$	○	○	○	○
59.		$	○	○	○	○
60.		$	○	○	○	○
61.		$	○	○	○	○
62.		$	○	○	○	○
63.		$	○	○	○	○

Bills & Payments

ORGANIZE, PLAN AND TRACK
MONTHLY BILLS, EXPENSES & PAYMENTS

Monthly Bills Calendar

YEAR

JAN
FEB
MAR
APR
MAY
JUN
JUL
AUG
SEP
OCT
NOV
DEC

SUN	MON	TUE	WED	THU	FRI	SAT

INCOME OVERVIEW

DATE	INCOME SOURCE	AMOUNT
	TOTAL INCOME:	

THIS MONTH'S FINANCIAL SUMMARY

TOTAL INCOME:	
TOTAL BILLS:	
OTHER EXPENSES:	
SAVINGS:	
NET REMAINING:	

Notes

• Bills & Payments •

PAID	BILL TO BE PAID	DATE DUE	AMOUNT DUE	AMOUNT PAID	UNPAID BALANCE	Notes
○			$	$	$	
○			$	$	$	
○			$	$	$	
○			$	$	$	
○			$	$	$	
○			$	$	$	
○			$	$	$	
○			$	$	$	
○			$	$	$	
○			$	$	$	
○			$	$	$	
○			$	$	$	
○			$	$	$	
○			$	$	$	
○			$	$	$	
○			$	$	$	
○			$	$	$	
○			$	$	$	
○			$	$	$	
○			$	$	$	
		TOTAL	$	$	$	

Monthly Bills Calendar

YEAR

JAN
FEB
MAR
APR
MAY
JUN
JUL
AUG
SEP
OCT
NOV
DEC

SUN	MON	TUE	WED	THU	FRI	SAT

INCOME OVERVIEW

DATE	INCOME SOURCE	AMOUNT
	TOTAL INCOME:	

THIS MONTH'S FINANCIAL SUMMARY

TOTAL INCOME:	
TOTAL BILLS:	
OTHER EXPENSES:	
SAVINGS:	
NET REMAINING:	

Notes

• Bills & Payments •

PAID	BILL TO BE PAID	DATE DUE	AMOUNT DUE	AMOUNT PAID	UNPAID BALANCE	Notes
○			$	$	$	
○			$	$	$	
○			$	$	$	
○			$	$	$	
○			$	$	$	
○			$	$	$	
○			$	$	$	
○			$	$	$	
○			$	$	$	
○			$	$	$	
○			$	$	$	
○			$	$	$	
○			$	$	$	
○			$	$	$	
○			$	$	$	
○			$	$	$	
○			$	$	$	
○			$	$	$	
○			$	$	$	
○			$	$	$	
		TOTAL	$	$	$	

Monthly Bills Calendar

YEAR

JAN
FEB
MAR
APR
MAY
JUN
JUL
AUG
SEP
OCT
NOV
DEC

SUN	MON	TUE	WED	THU	FRI	SAT

INCOME OVERVIEW

DATE	INCOME SOURCE	AMOUNT
	TOTAL INCOME:	

THIS MONTH'S FINANCIAL SUMMARY

TOTAL INCOME:	
TOTAL BILLS:	
OTHER EXPENSES:	
SAVINGS:	
NET REMAINING:	

Notes

• Bills & Payments •

PAID	BILL TO BE PAID	DATE DUE	AMOUNT DUE	AMOUNT PAID	UNPAID BALANCE	Notes
◯			$	$	$	
◯			$	$	$	
◯			$	$	$	
◯			$	$	$	
◯			$	$	$	
◯			$	$	$	
◯			$	$	$	
◯			$	$	$	
◯			$	$	$	
◯			$	$	$	
◯			$	$	$	
◯			$	$	$	
◯			$	$	$	
◯			$	$	$	
◯			$	$	$	
◯			$	$	$	
◯			$	$	$	
◯			$	$	$	
◯			$	$	$	
◯			$	$	$	
		TOTAL	$	$	$	

Monthly Bills Calendar

YEAR

JAN
FEB
MAR
APR
MAY
JUN
JUL
AUG
SEP
OCT
NOV
DEC

SUN	MON	TUE	WED	THU	FRI	SAT

INCOME OVERVIEW

DATE	INCOME SOURCE	AMOUNT
	TOTAL INCOME:	

THIS MONTH'S FINANCIAL SUMMARY

TOTAL INCOME:	
TOTAL BILLS:	
OTHER EXPENSES:	
SAVINGS:	
NET REMAINING:	

Notes

• Bills & Payments •

PAID	BILL TO BE PAID	DATE DUE	AMOUNT DUE	AMOUNT PAID	UNPAID BALANCE	Notes
○			$	$	$	
○			$	$	$	
○			$	$	$	
○			$	$	$	
○			$	$	$	
○			$	$	$	
○			$	$	$	
○			$	$	$	
○			$	$	$	
○			$	$	$	
○			$	$	$	
○			$	$	$	
○			$	$	$	
○			$	$	$	
○			$	$	$	
○			$	$	$	
○			$	$	$	
○			$	$	$	
○			$	$	$	
○			$	$	$	
		TOTAL	$	$	$	

Monthly Bills Calendar

YEAR

JAN FEB MAR APR MAY JUN JUL AUG SEP OCT NOV DEC

SUN	MON	TUE	WED	THU	FRI	SAT

INCOME OVERVIEW

DATE	INCOME SOURCE	AMOUNT
	TOTAL INCOME:	

THIS MONTH'S FINANCIAL SUMMARY

TOTAL INCOME:	
TOTAL BILLS:	
OTHER EXPENSES:	
SAVINGS:	
NET REMAINING:	

Notes

• Bills & Payments •

PAID	BILL TO BE PAID	DATE DUE	AMOUNT DUE	AMOUNT PAID	UNPAID BALANCE	Notes
○			$	$	$	
○			$	$	$	
○			$	$	$	
○			$	$	$	
○			$	$	$	
○			$	$	$	
○			$	$	$	
○			$	$	$	
○			$	$	$	
○			$	$	$	
○			$	$	$	
○			$	$	$	
○			$	$	$	
○			$	$	$	
○			$	$	$	
○			$	$	$	
○			$	$	$	
○			$	$	$	
○			$	$	$	
○			$	$	$	
		TOTAL	$	$	$	

Monthly Bills Calendar

YEAR

JAN FEB MAR APR MAY JUN JUL AUG SEP OCT NOV DEC

SUN	MON	TUE	WED	THU	FRI	SAT

INCOME OVERVIEW

DATE	INCOME SOURCE	AMOUNT
	TOTAL INCOME:	

THIS MONTH'S FINANCIAL SUMMARY

TOTAL INCOME:	
TOTAL BILLS:	
OTHER EXPENSES:	
SAVINGS:	
NET REMAINING:	

Notes

• Bills & Payments •

PAID	BILL TO BE PAID	DATE DUE	AMOUNT DUE	AMOUNT PAID	UNPAID BALANCE	Notes
○			$	$	$	
○			$	$	$	
○			$	$	$	
○			$	$	$	
○			$	$	$	
○			$	$	$	
○			$	$	$	
○			$	$	$	
○			$	$	$	
○			$	$	$	
○			$	$	$	
○			$	$	$	
○			$	$	$	
○			$	$	$	
○			$	$	$	
○			$	$	$	
○			$	$	$	
○			$	$	$	
○			$	$	$	
○			$	$	$	
		TOTAL	$	$	$	

Monthly Bills Calendar

YEAR

JAN FEB MAR APR MAY JUN JUL AUG SEP OCT NOV DEC

SUN	MON	TUE	WED	THU	FRI	SAT

INCOME OVERVIEW

DATE	INCOME SOURCE	AMOUNT
	TOTAL INCOME:	

THIS MONTH'S FINANCIAL SUMMARY

TOTAL INCOME:	
TOTAL BILLS:	
OTHER EXPENSES:	
SAVINGS:	
NET REMAINING:	

Notes

• Bills & Payments •

PAID	BILL TO BE PAID	DATE DUE	AMOUNT DUE	AMOUNT PAID	UNPAID BALANCE	Notes
○			$	$	$	
○			$	$	$	
○			$	$	$	
○			$	$	$	
○			$	$	$	
○			$	$	$	
○			$	$	$	
○			$	$	$	
○			$	$	$	
○			$	$	$	
○			$	$	$	
○			$	$	$	
○			$	$	$	
○			$	$	$	
○			$	$	$	
○			$	$	$	
○			$	$	$	
○			$	$	$	
○			$	$	$	
○			$	$	$	
		TOTAL	$	$	$	

Monthly Bills Calendar

YEAR

JAN
FEB
MAR
APR
MAY
JUN
JUL
AUG
SEP
OCT
NOV
DEC

SUN	MON	TUE	WED	THU	FRI	SAT

INCOME OVERVIEW

DATE	INCOME SOURCE	AMOUNT
	TOTAL INCOME:	

THIS MONTH'S FINANCIAL SUMMARY

TOTAL INCOME:	
TOTAL BILLS:	
OTHER EXPENSES:	
SAVINGS:	
NET REMAINING:	

Notes

• Bills & Payments •

PAID	BILL TO BE PAID	DATE DUE	AMOUNT DUE	AMOUNT PAID	UNPAID BALANCE	Notes
○			$	$	$	
○			$	$	$	
○			$	$	$	
○			$	$	$	
○			$	$	$	
○			$	$	$	
○			$	$	$	
○			$	$	$	
○			$	$	$	
○			$	$	$	
○			$	$	$	
○			$	$	$	
○			$	$	$	
○			$	$	$	
○			$	$	$	
○			$	$	$	
○			$	$	$	
○			$	$	$	
○			$	$	$	
○			$	$	$	
		TOTAL	$	$	$	

Monthly Bills Calendar

YEAR

JAN FEB MAR APR MAY JUN JUL AUG SEP OCT NOV DEC

SUN	MON	TUE	WED	THU	FRI	SAT

INCOME OVERVIEW

DATE	INCOME SOURCE	AMOUNT
	TOTAL INCOME:	

THIS MONTH'S FINANCIAL SUMMARY

TOTAL INCOME:	
TOTAL BILLS:	
OTHER EXPENSES:	
SAVINGS:	
NET REMAINING:	

Notes

• Bills & Payments •

PAID	BILL TO BE PAID	DATE DUE	AMOUNT DUE	AMOUNT PAID	UNPAID BALANCE	Notes
○			$	$	$	
○			$	$	$	
○			$	$	$	
○			$	$	$	
○			$	$	$	
○			$	$	$	
○			$	$	$	
○			$	$	$	
○			$	$	$	
○			$	$	$	
○			$	$	$	
○			$	$	$	
○			$	$	$	
○			$	$	$	
○			$	$	$	
○			$	$	$	
○			$	$	$	
○			$	$	$	
○			$	$	$	
○			$	$	$	
		TOTAL	$	$	$	

Monthly Bills Calendar

YEAR

JAN FEB MAR APR MAY JUN JUL AUG SEP OCT NOV DEC

SUN	MON	TUE	WED	THU	FRI	SAT

INCOME OVERVIEW

DATE	INCOME SOURCE	AMOUNT
	TOTAL INCOME:	

THIS MONTH'S FINANCIAL SUMMARY

TOTAL INCOME:	
TOTAL BILLS:	
OTHER EXPENSES:	
SAVINGS:	
NET REMAINING:	

Notes

• Bills & Payments •

PAID	BILL TO BE PAID	DATE DUE	AMOUNT DUE	AMOUNT PAID	UNPAID BALANCE	Notes
○			$	$	$	
○			$	$	$	
○			$	$	$	
○			$	$	$	
○			$	$	$	
○			$	$	$	
○			$	$	$	
○			$	$	$	
○			$	$	$	
○			$	$	$	
○			$	$	$	
○			$	$	$	
○			$	$	$	
○			$	$	$	
○			$	$	$	
○			$	$	$	
○			$	$	$	
○			$	$	$	
○			$	$	$	
○			$	$	$	
		TOTAL	$	$	$	

Monthly Bills Calendar

YEAR

JAN FEB MAR APR MAY JUN JUL AUG SEP OCT NOV DEC

SUN	MON	TUE	WED	THU	FRI	SAT

INCOME OVERVIEW

DATE	INCOME SOURCE	AMOUNT
	TOTAL INCOME:	

THIS MONTH'S FINANCIAL SUMMARY

TOTAL INCOME:	
TOTAL BILLS:	
OTHER EXPENSES:	
SAVINGS:	
NET REMAINING:	

Notes

• Bills & Payments •

PAID	BILL TO BE PAID	DATE DUE	AMOUNT DUE	AMOUNT PAID	UNPAID BALANCE	Notes
○			$	$	$	
○			$	$	$	
○			$	$	$	
○			$	$	$	
○			$	$	$	
○			$	$	$	
○			$	$	$	
○			$	$	$	
○			$	$	$	
○			$	$	$	
○			$	$	$	
○			$	$	$	
○			$	$	$	
○			$	$	$	
○			$	$	$	
○			$	$	$	
○			$	$	$	
○			$	$	$	
○			$	$	$	
○			$	$	$	
TOTAL			$	$	$	

Monthly Bills Calendar

YEAR

JAN FEB MAR APR MAY JUN JUL AUG SEP OCT NOV DEC

SUN	MON	TUE	WED	THU	FRI	SAT

INCOME OVERVIEW

DATE	INCOME SOURCE	AMOUNT
	TOTAL INCOME:	

THIS MONTH'S FINANCIAL SUMMARY

TOTAL INCOME:	
TOTAL BILLS:	
OTHER EXPENSES:	
SAVINGS:	
NET REMAINING:	

Notes

• Bills & Payments •

PAID	BILL TO BE PAID	DATE DUE	AMOUNT DUE	AMOUNT PAID	UNPAID BALANCE	Notes
○			$	$	$	
○			$	$	$	
○			$	$	$	
○			$	$	$	
○			$	$	$	
○			$	$	$	
○			$	$	$	
○			$	$	$	
○			$	$	$	
○			$	$	$	
○			$	$	$	
○			$	$	$	
○			$	$	$	
○			$	$	$	
○			$	$	$	
○			$	$	$	
○			$	$	$	
○			$	$	$	
○			$	$	$	
○			$	$	$	
		TOTAL	$	$	$	

Monthly Bills Calendar

YEAR

JAN FEB MAR APR MAY JUN JUL AUG SEP OCT NOV DEC

SUN	MON	TUE	WED	THU	FRI	SAT

INCOME OVERVIEW

DATE	INCOME SOURCE	AMOUNT
	TOTAL INCOME:	

THIS MONTH'S FINANCIAL SUMMARY

TOTAL INCOME:	
TOTAL BILLS:	
OTHER EXPENSES:	
SAVINGS:	
NET REMAINING:	

Notes

• Bills & Payments •

PAID	BILL TO BE PAID	DATE DUE	AMOUNT DUE	AMOUNT PAID	UNPAID BALANCE	Notes
○			$	$	$	
○			$	$	$	
○			$	$	$	
○			$	$	$	
○			$	$	$	
○			$	$	$	
○			$	$	$	
○			$	$	$	
○			$	$	$	
○			$	$	$	
○			$	$	$	
○			$	$	$	
○			$	$	$	
○			$	$	$	
○			$	$	$	
○			$	$	$	
○			$	$	$	
○			$	$	$	
○			$	$	$	
○			$	$	$	
		TOTAL	$	$	$	

Monthly Bills Calendar

YEAR

JAN
FEB
MAR
APR
MAY
JUN
JUL
AUG
SEP
OCT
NOV
DEC

SUN	MON	TUE	WED	THU	FRI	SAT

INCOME OVERVIEW

DATE	INCOME SOURCE	AMOUNT
	TOTAL INCOME:	

THIS MONTH'S FINANCIAL SUMMARY

TOTAL INCOME:	
TOTAL BILLS:	
OTHER EXPENSES:	
SAVINGS:	
NET REMAINING:	

Notes

• Bills & Payments •

PAID	BILL TO BE PAID	DATE DUE	AMOUNT DUE	AMOUNT PAID	UNPAID BALANCE	Notes
○			$	$	$	
○			$	$	$	
○			$	$	$	
○			$	$	$	
○			$	$	$	
○			$	$	$	
○			$	$	$	
○			$	$	$	
○			$	$	$	
○			$	$	$	
○			$	$	$	
○			$	$	$	
○			$	$	$	
○			$	$	$	
○			$	$	$	
○			$	$	$	
○			$	$	$	
○			$	$	$	
○			$	$	$	
○			$	$	$	
		TOTAL	$	$	$	

Monthly Bills Calendar

YEAR

JAN FEB MAR APR MAY JUN JUL AUG SEP OCT NOV DEC

SUN	MON	TUE	WED	THU	FRI	SAT

INCOME OVERVIEW

DATE	INCOME SOURCE	AMOUNT
	TOTAL INCOME:	

THIS MONTH'S FINANCIAL SUMMARY

TOTAL INCOME:	
TOTAL BILLS:	
OTHER EXPENSES:	
SAVINGS:	
NET REMAINING:	

Notes

• Bills & Payments •

PAID	BILL TO BE PAID	DATE DUE	AMOUNT DUE	AMOUNT PAID	UNPAID BALANCE	Notes
○			$	$	$	
○			$	$	$	
○			$	$	$	
○			$	$	$	
○			$	$	$	
○			$	$	$	
○			$	$	$	
○			$	$	$	
○			$	$	$	
○			$	$	$	
○			$	$	$	
○			$	$	$	
○			$	$	$	
○			$	$	$	
○			$	$	$	
○			$	$	$	
○			$	$	$	
○			$	$	$	
○			$	$	$	
○			$	$	$	
		TOTAL	$	$	$	

Monthly Bills Calendar

YEAR

JAN FEB MAR APR MAY JUN JUL AUG SEP OCT NOV DEC

SUN	MON	TUE	WED	THU	FRI	SAT

INCOME OVERVIEW

DATE	INCOME SOURCE	AMOUNT
	TOTAL INCOME:	

THIS MONTH'S FINANCIAL SUMMARY

TOTAL INCOME:	
TOTAL BILLS:	
OTHER EXPENSES:	
SAVINGS:	
NET REMAINING:	

Notes

• Bills & Payments •

PAID	BILL TO BE PAID	DATE DUE	AMOUNT DUE	AMOUNT PAID	UNPAID BALANCE	Notes
○			$	$	$	
○			$	$	$	
○			$	$	$	
○			$	$	$	
○			$	$	$	
○			$	$	$	
○			$	$	$	
○			$	$	$	
○			$	$	$	
○			$	$	$	
○			$	$	$	
○			$	$	$	
○			$	$	$	
○			$	$	$	
○			$	$	$	
○			$	$	$	
○			$	$	$	
○			$	$	$	
○			$	$	$	
○			$	$	$	
		TOTAL	$	$	$	

Monthly Bills Calendar

YEAR

JAN FEB MAR APR MAY JUN JUL AUG SEP OCT NOV DEC

SUN	MON	TUE	WED	THU	FRI	SAT

INCOME OVERVIEW

DATE	INCOME SOURCE	AMOUNT
	TOTAL INCOME:	

THIS MONTH'S FINANCIAL SUMMARY

TOTAL INCOME:	
TOTAL BILLS:	
OTHER EXPENSES:	
SAVINGS:	
NET REMAINING:	

Notes

• Bills & Payments •

PAID	BILL TO BE PAID	DATE DUE	AMOUNT DUE	AMOUNT PAID	UNPAID BALANCE	Notes
◯			$	$	$	
◯			$	$	$	
◯			$	$	$	
◯			$	$	$	
◯			$	$	$	
◯			$	$	$	
◯			$	$	$	
◯			$	$	$	
◯			$	$	$	
◯			$	$	$	
◯			$	$	$	
◯			$	$	$	
◯			$	$	$	
◯			$	$	$	
◯			$	$	$	
◯			$	$	$	
◯			$	$	$	
◯			$	$	$	
◯			$	$	$	
◯			$	$	$	
TOTAL			$	$	$	

Monthly Bills Calendar

YEAR

JAN FEB MAR APR MAY JUN JUL AUG SEP OCT NOV DEC

SUN	MON	TUE	WED	THU	FRI	SAT

INCOME OVERVIEW

DATE	INCOME SOURCE	AMOUNT
	TOTAL INCOME:	

THIS MONTH'S FINANCIAL SUMMARY

TOTAL INCOME:	
TOTAL BILLS:	
OTHER EXPENSES:	
SAVINGS:	
NET REMAINING:	

Notes

• Bills & Payments •

PAID	BILL TO BE PAID	DATE DUE	AMOUNT DUE	AMOUNT PAID	UNPAID BALANCE	Notes
○			$	$	$	
○			$	$	$	
○			$	$	$	
○			$	$	$	
○			$	$	$	
○			$	$	$	
○			$	$	$	
○			$	$	$	
○			$	$	$	
○			$	$	$	
○			$	$	$	
○			$	$	$	
○			$	$	$	
○			$	$	$	
○			$	$	$	
○			$	$	$	
○			$	$	$	
○			$	$	$	
○			$	$	$	
○			$	$	$	
		TOTAL	$	$	$	

Monthly Bills Calendar

YEAR

JAN FEB MAR APR MAY JUN JUL AUG SEP OCT NOV DEC

SUN	MON	TUE	WED	THU	FRI	SAT

INCOME OVERVIEW

DATE	INCOME SOURCE	AMOUNT
	TOTAL INCOME:	

THIS MONTH'S FINANCIAL SUMMARY

TOTAL INCOME:	
TOTAL BILLS:	
OTHER EXPENSES:	
SAVINGS:	
NET REMAINING:	

Notes

• Bills & Payments •

PAID	BILL TO BE PAID	DATE DUE	AMOUNT DUE	AMOUNT PAID	UNPAID BALANCE	Notes
○			$	$	$	
○			$	$	$	
○			$	$	$	
○			$	$	$	
○			$	$	$	
○			$	$	$	
○			$	$	$	
○			$	$	$	
○			$	$	$	
○			$	$	$	
○			$	$	$	
○			$	$	$	
○			$	$	$	
○			$	$	$	
○			$	$	$	
○			$	$	$	
○			$	$	$	
○			$	$	$	
○			$	$	$	
○			$	$	$	
		TOTAL	$	$	$	

Monthly Bills Calendar

YEAR

JAN
FEB
MAR
APR
MAY
JUN
JUL
AUG
SEP
OCT
NOV
DEC

SUN	MON	TUE	WED	THU	FRI	SAT

INCOME OVERVIEW

DATE	INCOME SOURCE	AMOUNT
	TOTAL INCOME:	

THIS MONTH'S FINANCIAL SUMMARY

TOTAL INCOME:	
TOTAL BILLS:	
OTHER EXPENSES:	
SAVINGS:	
NET REMAINING:	

Notes

• Bills & Payments •

PAID	BILL TO BE PAID	DATE DUE	AMOUNT DUE	AMOUNT PAID	UNPAID BALANCE	Notes
○			$	$	$	
○			$	$	$	
○			$	$	$	
○			$	$	$	
○			$	$	$	
○			$	$	$	
○			$	$	$	
○			$	$	$	
○			$	$	$	
○			$	$	$	
○			$	$	$	
○			$	$	$	
○			$	$	$	
○			$	$	$	
○			$	$	$	
○			$	$	$	
○			$	$	$	
○			$	$	$	
○			$	$	$	
○			$	$	$	
		TOTAL	$	$	$	

Monthly Bills Calendar

YEAR

JAN FEB MAR APR MAY JUN JUL AUG SEP OCT NOV DEC

SUN	MON	TUE	WED	THU	FRI	SAT

INCOME OVERVIEW

DATE	INCOME SOURCE	AMOUNT
	TOTAL INCOME:	

THIS MONTH'S FINANCIAL SUMMARY

TOTAL INCOME:	
TOTAL BILLS:	
OTHER EXPENSES:	
SAVINGS:	
NET REMAINING:	

Notes

• Bills & Payments •

PAID	BILL TO BE PAID	DATE DUE	AMOUNT DUE	AMOUNT PAID	UNPAID BALANCE	Notes
			$	$	$	
			$	$	$	
			$	$	$	
			$	$	$	
			$	$	$	
			$	$	$	
			$	$	$	
			$	$	$	
			$	$	$	
			$	$	$	
			$	$	$	
			$	$	$	
			$	$	$	
			$	$	$	
			$	$	$	
			$	$	$	
			$	$	$	
			$	$	$	
			$	$	$	
			$	$	$	
		TOTAL	$	$	$	

Monthly Bills Calendar

YEAR

	SUN	MON	TUE	WED	THU	FRI	SAT
JAN							
FEB							
MAR							
APR							
MAY							
JUN							
JUL							
AUG							
SEP							
OCT							
NOV							
DEC							

INCOME OVERVIEW

DATE	INCOME SOURCE	AMOUNT
	TOTAL INCOME:	

THIS MONTH'S FINANCIAL SUMMARY

TOTAL INCOME:	
TOTAL BILLS:	
OTHER EXPENSES:	
SAVINGS:	
NET REMAINING:	

Notes

• Bills & Payments •

PAID	BILL TO BE PAID	DATE DUE	AMOUNT DUE	AMOUNT PAID	UNPAID BALANCE	Notes
◯			$	$	$	
◯			$	$	$	
◯			$	$	$	
◯			$	$	$	
◯			$	$	$	
◯			$	$	$	
◯			$	$	$	
◯			$	$	$	
◯			$	$	$	
◯			$	$	$	
◯			$	$	$	
◯			$	$	$	
◯			$	$	$	
◯			$	$	$	
◯			$	$	$	
◯			$	$	$	
◯			$	$	$	
◯			$	$	$	
◯			$	$	$	
◯			$	$	$	
		TOTAL	$	$	$	

Monthly Bills Calendar

YEAR

	SUN	MON	TUE	WED	THU	FRI	SAT
JAN							
FEB							
MAR							
APR							
MAY							
JUN							
JUL							
AUG							
SEP							
OCT							
NOV							
DEC							

INCOME OVERVIEW

DATE	INCOME SOURCE	AMOUNT
	TOTAL INCOME:	

THIS MONTH'S FINANCIAL SUMMARY

TOTAL INCOME:	
TOTAL BILLS:	
OTHER EXPENSES:	
SAVINGS:	
NET REMAINING:	

Notes

• Bills & Payments •

PAID	BILL TO BE PAID	DATE DUE	AMOUNT DUE	AMOUNT PAID	UNPAID BALANCE	Notes
○			$	$	$	
○			$	$	$	
○			$	$	$	
○			$	$	$	
○			$	$	$	
○			$	$	$	
○			$	$	$	
○			$	$	$	
○			$	$	$	
○			$	$	$	
○			$	$	$	
○			$	$	$	
○			$	$	$	
○			$	$	$	
○			$	$	$	
○			$	$	$	
○			$	$	$	
○			$	$	$	
○			$	$	$	
○			$	$	$	
		TOTAL	$	$	$	

Monthly Bills Calendar

YEAR

JAN FEB MAR APR MAY JUN JUL AUG SEP OCT NOV DEC

SUN	MON	TUE	WED	THU	FRI	SAT

INCOME OVERVIEW

DATE	INCOME SOURCE	AMOUNT
	TOTAL INCOME:	

THIS MONTH'S FINANCIAL SUMMARY

TOTAL INCOME:	
TOTAL BILLS:	
OTHER EXPENSES:	
SAVINGS:	
NET REMAINING:	

Notes

• Bills & Payments •

PAID	BILL TO BE PAID	DATE DUE	AMOUNT DUE	AMOUNT PAID	UNPAID BALANCE	Notes
○			$	$	$	
○			$	$	$	
○			$	$	$	
○			$	$	$	
○			$	$	$	
○			$	$	$	
○			$	$	$	
○			$	$	$	
○			$	$	$	
○			$	$	$	
○			$	$	$	
○			$	$	$	
○			$	$	$	
○			$	$	$	
○			$	$	$	
○			$	$	$	
○			$	$	$	
○			$	$	$	
○			$	$	$	
○			$	$	$	
		TOTAL	$	$	$	

Monthly Bills Calendar

YEAR

JAN FEB MAR APR MAY JUN JUL AUG SEP OCT NOV DEC

SUN	MON	TUE	WED	THU	FRI	SAT

INCOME OVERVIEW

DATE	INCOME SOURCE	AMOUNT
	TOTAL INCOME:	

THIS MONTH'S FINANCIAL SUMMARY

TOTAL INCOME:	
TOTAL BILLS:	
OTHER EXPENSES:	
SAVINGS:	
NET REMAINING:	

Notes

• Bills & Payments •

PAID	BILL TO BE PAID	DATE DUE	AMOUNT DUE	AMOUNT PAID	UNPAID BALANCE	Notes
◯			$	$	$	
◯			$	$	$	
◯			$	$	$	
◯			$	$	$	
◯			$	$	$	
◯			$	$	$	
◯			$	$	$	
◯			$	$	$	
◯			$	$	$	
◯			$	$	$	
◯			$	$	$	
◯			$	$	$	
◯			$	$	$	
◯			$	$	$	
◯			$	$	$	
◯			$	$	$	
◯			$	$	$	
◯			$	$	$	
◯			$	$	$	
◯			$	$	$	
		TOTAL	$	$	$	

Monthly Bills Calendar

YEAR

JAN
FEB
MAR
APR
MAY
JUN
JUL
AUG
SEP
OCT
NOV
DEC

SUN	MON	TUE	WED	THU	FRI	SAT

INCOME OVERVIEW

DATE	INCOME SOURCE	AMOUNT
	TOTAL INCOME:	

THIS MONTH'S FINANCIAL SUMMARY

TOTAL INCOME:	
TOTAL BILLS:	
OTHER EXPENSES:	
SAVINGS:	
NET REMAINING:	

Notes

• Bills & Payments •

PAID	BILL TO BE PAID	DATE DUE	AMOUNT DUE	AMOUNT PAID	UNPAID BALANCE	Notes
○			$	$	$	
○			$	$	$	
○			$	$	$	
○			$	$	$	
○			$	$	$	
○			$	$	$	
○			$	$	$	
○			$	$	$	
○			$	$	$	
○			$	$	$	
○			$	$	$	
○			$	$	$	
○			$	$	$	
○			$	$	$	
○			$	$	$	
○			$	$	$	
○			$	$	$	
○			$	$	$	
○			$	$	$	
○			$	$	$	
TOTAL			$	$	$	

Monthly Bills Calendar

YEAR

JAN FEB MAR APR MAY JUN JUL AUG SEP OCT NOV DEC

SUN	MON	TUE	WED	THU	FRI	SAT

INCOME OVERVIEW

DATE	INCOME SOURCE	AMOUNT
	TOTAL INCOME:	

THIS MONTH'S FINANCIAL SUMMARY

TOTAL INCOME:	
TOTAL BILLS:	
OTHER EXPENSES:	
SAVINGS:	
NET REMAINING:	

Notes

• Bills & Payments •

PAID	BILL TO BE PAID	DATE DUE	AMOUNT DUE	AMOUNT PAID	UNPAID BALANCE	Notes
○			$	$	$	
○			$	$	$	
○			$	$	$	
○			$	$	$	
○			$	$	$	
○			$	$	$	
○			$	$	$	
○			$	$	$	
○			$	$	$	
○			$	$	$	
○			$	$	$	
○			$	$	$	
○			$	$	$	
○			$	$	$	
○			$	$	$	
○			$	$	$	
○			$	$	$	
○			$	$	$	
○			$	$	$	
○			$	$	$	
		TOTAL	$	$	$	

Monthly Bills Calendar

YEAR

JAN FEB MAR APR MAY JUN JUL AUG SEP OCT NOV DEC

SUN	MON	TUE	WED	THU	FRI	SAT

INCOME OVERVIEW

DATE	INCOME SOURCE	AMOUNT
	TOTAL INCOME:	

THIS MONTH'S FINANCIAL SUMMARY

TOTAL INCOME:	
TOTAL BILLS:	
OTHER EXPENSES:	
SAVINGS:	
NET REMAINING:	

Notes

• Bills & Payments •

PAID	BILL TO BE PAID	DATE DUE	AMOUNT DUE	AMOUNT PAID	UNPAID BALANCE	Notes
○			$	$	$	
○			$	$	$	
○			$	$	$	
○			$	$	$	
○			$	$	$	
○			$	$	$	
○			$	$	$	
○			$	$	$	
○			$	$	$	
○			$	$	$	
○			$	$	$	
○			$	$	$	
○			$	$	$	
○			$	$	$	
○			$	$	$	
○			$	$	$	
○			$	$	$	
○			$	$	$	
○			$	$	$	
○			$	$	$	
		TOTAL	$	$	$	

Monthly Bills Calendar

YEAR

JAN FEB MAR APR MAY JUN JUL AUG SEP OCT NOV DEC

SUN	MON	TUE	WED	THU	FRI	SAT

INCOME OVERVIEW

DATE	INCOME SOURCE	AMOUNT
	TOTAL INCOME:	

THIS MONTH'S FINANCIAL SUMMARY

TOTAL INCOME:	
TOTAL BILLS:	
OTHER EXPENSES:	
SAVINGS:	
NET REMAINING:	

Notes

• Bills & Payments •

PAID	BILL TO BE PAID	DATE DUE	AMOUNT DUE	AMOUNT PAID	UNPAID BALANCE	Notes
○			$	$	$	
○			$	$	$	
○			$	$	$	
○			$	$	$	
○			$	$	$	
○			$	$	$	
○			$	$	$	
○			$	$	$	
○			$	$	$	
○			$	$	$	
○			$	$	$	
○			$	$	$	
○			$	$	$	
○			$	$	$	
○			$	$	$	
○			$	$	$	
○			$	$	$	
○			$	$	$	
○			$	$	$	
○			$	$	$	
		TOTAL	$	$	$	

Monthly Bills Calendar

YEAR

JAN
FEB
MAR
APR
MAY
JUN
JUL
AUG
SEP
OCT
NOV
DEC

SUN	MON	TUE	WED	THU	FRI	SAT

INCOME OVERVIEW

DATE	INCOME SOURCE	AMOUNT
	TOTAL INCOME:	

THIS MONTH'S FINANCIAL SUMMARY

TOTAL INCOME:	
TOTAL BILLS:	
OTHER EXPENSES:	
SAVINGS:	
NET REMAINING:	

Notes

• Bills & Payments •

PAID	BILL TO BE PAID	DATE DUE	AMOUNT DUE	AMOUNT PAID	UNPAID BALANCE	Notes
○			$	$	$	
○			$	$	$	
○			$	$	$	
○			$	$	$	
○			$	$	$	
○			$	$	$	
○			$	$	$	
○			$	$	$	
○			$	$	$	
○			$	$	$	
○			$	$	$	
○			$	$	$	
○			$	$	$	
○			$	$	$	
○			$	$	$	
○			$	$	$	
○			$	$	$	
○			$	$	$	
○			$	$	$	
○			$	$	$	
		TOTAL	$	$	$	

Monthly Bills Calendar

YEAR

JAN FEB MAR APR MAY JUN JUL AUG SEP OCT NOV DEC

SUN	MON	TUE	WED	THU	FRI	SAT

INCOME OVERVIEW

DATE	INCOME SOURCE	AMOUNT
	TOTAL INCOME:	

THIS MONTH'S FINANCIAL SUMMARY

TOTAL INCOME:	
TOTAL BILLS:	
OTHER EXPENSES:	
SAVINGS:	
NET REMAINING:	

Notes

• Bills & Payments •

PAID	BILL TO BE PAID	DATE DUE	AMOUNT DUE	AMOUNT PAID	UNPAID BALANCE	Notes
○			$	$	$	
○			$	$	$	
○			$	$	$	
○			$	$	$	
○			$	$	$	
○			$	$	$	
○			$	$	$	
○			$	$	$	
○			$	$	$	
○			$	$	$	
○			$	$	$	
○			$	$	$	
○			$	$	$	
○			$	$	$	
○			$	$	$	
○			$	$	$	
○			$	$	$	
○			$	$	$	
○			$	$	$	
○			$	$	$	
		TOTAL	$	$	$	

Monthly Bills Calendar

YEAR

JAN FEB MAR APR MAY JUN JUL AUG SEP OCT NOV DEC

SUN	MON	TUE	WED	THU	FRI	SAT

INCOME OVERVIEW

DATE	INCOME SOURCE	AMOUNT
	TOTAL INCOME:	

THIS MONTH'S FINANCIAL SUMMARY

TOTAL INCOME:	
TOTAL BILLS:	
OTHER EXPENSES:	
SAVINGS:	
NET REMAINING:	

Notes

• Bills & Payments •

PAID	BILL TO BE PAID	DATE DUE	AMOUNT DUE	AMOUNT PAID	UNPAID BALANCE	Notes
○			$	$	$	
○			$	$	$	
○			$	$	$	
○			$	$	$	
○			$	$	$	
○			$	$	$	
○			$	$	$	
○			$	$	$	
○			$	$	$	
○			$	$	$	
○			$	$	$	
○			$	$	$	
○			$	$	$	
○			$	$	$	
○			$	$	$	
○			$	$	$	
○			$	$	$	
○			$	$	$	
○			$	$	$	
○			$	$	$	
		TOTAL	$	$	$	

Monthly Bills Calendar

YEAR

JAN FEB MAR APR MAY JUN JUL AUG SEP OCT NOV DEC

SUN	MON	TUE	WED	THU	FRI	SAT

INCOME OVERVIEW

DATE	INCOME SOURCE	AMOUNT
	TOTAL INCOME:	

THIS MONTH'S FINANCIAL SUMMARY

TOTAL INCOME:	
TOTAL BILLS:	
OTHER EXPENSES:	
SAVINGS:	
NET REMAINING:	

Notes

• Bills & Payments •

PAID	BILL TO BE PAID	DATE DUE	AMOUNT DUE	AMOUNT PAID	UNPAID BALANCE	Notes
○			$	$	$	
○			$	$	$	
○			$	$	$	
○			$	$	$	
○			$	$	$	
○			$	$	$	
○			$	$	$	
○			$	$	$	
○			$	$	$	
○			$	$	$	
○			$	$	$	
○			$	$	$	
○			$	$	$	
○			$	$	$	
○			$	$	$	
○			$	$	$	
○			$	$	$	
○			$	$	$	
○			$	$	$	
○			$	$	$	
		TOTAL	$	$	$	

Monthly Bills Calendar

YEAR

JAN FEB MAR APR MAY JUN JUL AUG SEP OCT NOV DEC

SUN	MON	TUE	WED	THU	FRI	SAT

INCOME OVERVIEW

DATE	INCOME SOURCE	AMOUNT
	TOTAL INCOME:	

THIS MONTH'S FINANCIAL SUMMARY

TOTAL INCOME:	
TOTAL BILLS:	
OTHER EXPENSES:	
SAVINGS:	
NET REMAINING:	

Notes

• Bills & Payments •

PAID	BILL TO BE PAID	DATE DUE	AMOUNT DUE	AMOUNT PAID	UNPAID BALANCE	Notes
○			$	$	$	
○			$	$	$	
○			$	$	$	
○			$	$	$	
○			$	$	$	
○			$	$	$	
○			$	$	$	
○			$	$	$	
○			$	$	$	
○			$	$	$	
○			$	$	$	
○			$	$	$	
○			$	$	$	
○			$	$	$	
○			$	$	$	
○			$	$	$	
○			$	$	$	
○			$	$	$	
○			$	$	$	
○			$	$	$	
		TOTAL	$	$	$	

Monthly Bills Calendar

YEAR

JAN FEB MAR APR MAY JUN JUL AUG SEP OCT NOV DEC

SUN	MON	TUE	WED	THU	FRI	SAT

INCOME OVERVIEW

DATE	INCOME SOURCE	AMOUNT
	TOTAL INCOME:	

THIS MONTH'S FINANCIAL SUMMARY

TOTAL INCOME:	
TOTAL BILLS:	
OTHER EXPENSES:	
SAVINGS:	
NET REMAINING:	

Notes

• Bills & Payments •

PAID	BILL TO BE PAID	DATE DUE	AMOUNT DUE	AMOUNT PAID	UNPAID BALANCE	Notes
○			$	$	$	
○			$	$	$	
○			$	$	$	
○			$	$	$	
○			$	$	$	
○			$	$	$	
○			$	$	$	
○			$	$	$	
○			$	$	$	
○			$	$	$	
○			$	$	$	
○			$	$	$	
○			$	$	$	
○			$	$	$	
○			$	$	$	
○			$	$	$	
○			$	$	$	
○			$	$	$	
○			$	$	$	
○			$	$	$	
TOTAL			$	$	$	

Monthly Bills Calendar

YEAR

JAN
FEB
MAR
APR
MAY
JUN
JUL
AUG
SEP
OCT
NOV
DEC

SUN	MON	TUE	WED	THU	FRI	SAT

INCOME OVERVIEW

DATE	INCOME SOURCE	AMOUNT
	TOTAL INCOME:	

THIS MONTH'S FINANCIAL SUMMARY

TOTAL INCOME:	
TOTAL BILLS:	
OTHER EXPENSES:	
SAVINGS:	
NET REMAINING:	

Notes

• Bills & Payments •

PAID	BILL TO BE PAID	DATE DUE	AMOUNT DUE	AMOUNT PAID	UNPAID BALANCE	Notes
○			$	$	$	
○			$	$	$	
○			$	$	$	
○			$	$	$	
○			$	$	$	
○			$	$	$	
○			$	$	$	
○			$	$	$	
○			$	$	$	
○			$	$	$	
○			$	$	$	
○			$	$	$	
○			$	$	$	
○			$	$	$	
○			$	$	$	
○			$	$	$	
○			$	$	$	
○			$	$	$	
○			$	$	$	
○			$	$	$	
		TOTAL	$	$	$	

Debt Pay-Off Tracker

ORGANIZE, PLAN, AND TRACK YOUR DEBT-FREE FUTURE

• HOW TO USE THE DEBT-PAYOFF WORKSHEETS •

One of the more popular methods for paying off debt is known as the snowball method. This approach involves paying off your debts in order of smallest to largest, which can help you build momentum and motivation as you work toward becoming debt-free.

This section's worksheets are designed to assist you in applying this method. Or simply use them to track your balance if you follow any other strategies.

1. Use the **Payoff Priority Planner worksheet** to list all your debts from smallest to largest balance.

2. **Tackle your smallest debt first.**

   Pay as much as possible on the smallest debt (minimum due + extra) to pay it off as soon as you can.

   Minimum Due $ + Extra $ = New Payment $$ To Smallest Debt

   Continue to make minimum payments on all other debts.

3. Once the smallest debt is paid-off, roll that payment (minimum + extras) onto the next smallest debt on the list.

   Minimum Payment + Rollover = New Payment

4. Repeat until you are debt free!

PAY-OFF PRIORITY PLANNER

DEBT	BALANCE	MINIMUM PAYMENT	+	ROLLOVER	=	NEW PAYMENT	PAID OFF?
	$	$	+	$	=	$	
	$	$	+	$	=	$	
	$	$	+	$	=	$	
	$	$	+	$	=	$	
	$	$	+	$	=	$	
	$	$	+	$	=	$	
	$	$	+	$	=	$	
	$	$	+	$	=	$	
	$	$	+	$	=	$	
	$	$	+	$	=	$	
	$	$	+	$	=	$	
	$	$	+	$	=	$	
	$	$	+	$	=	$	
	$	$	+	$	=	$	
TOTAL	$	$					

PAY-OFF PRIORITY PLANNER

DEBT	BALANCE	MINIMUM PAYMENT	+	ROLLOVER	=	NEW PAYMENT	PAID OFF?
	$	$	+	$	=	$	○
	$	$	+	$	=	$	○
	$	$	+	$	=	$	○
	$	$	+	$	=	$	○
	$	$	+	$	=	$	○
	$	$	+	$	=	$	○
	$	$	+	$	=	$	○
	$	$	+	$	=	$	○
	$	$	+	$	=	$	○
	$	$	+	$	=	$	○
	$	$	+	$	=	$	○
	$	$	+	$	=	$	○
	$	$	+	$	=	$	○
	$	$	+	$	=	$	○
TOTAL	$	$					

DEBT PAY-OFF TRACKER

DEBT	CREDITOR
INTEREST RATE %	TERM
STARTING BALANCE $	PAYOFF DATE GOAL
MONTHLY PAYMENT MINIMUM $	MONTHLY PAYMENT GOAL $

• VISUAL TRACKER •

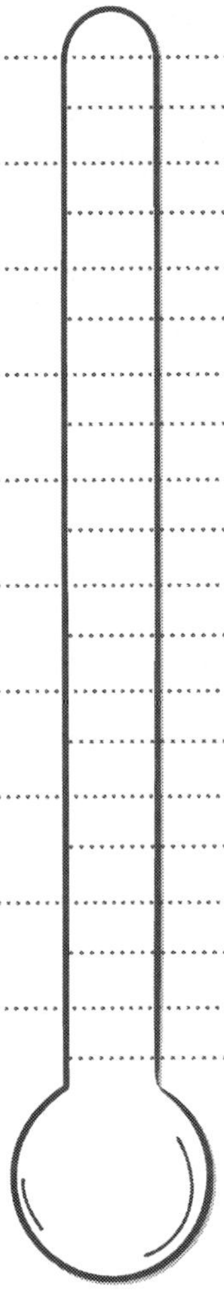

$ 100%

95%

$ 90%

85%

$ 80%

75%

$ 70%

65%

$ 60%

55%

$ 50%

45%

$ 40%

35%

$ 30%

25%

$ 20%

15%

$ 10%

5%

Color in the rows as you pay-off debt balance.

Notes

Debt Pay-off Tracker

DATE	PAYMENT	BALANCE	DATE	PAYMENT	BALANCE
	$	$		$	$
	$	$		$	$
	$	$		$	$
	$	$		$	$
	$	$		$	$
	$	$		$	$
	$	$		$	$
	$	$		$	$
	$	$		$	$
	$	$		$	$
	$	$		$	$
	$	$		$	$
	$	$		$	$
	$	$		$	$
	$	$		$	$
	$	$		$	$

Debt Pay-off Tracker

DEBT	CREDITOR
INTEREST RATE %	TERM
STARTING BALANCE $	PAYOFF DATE GOAL
MONTHLY PAYMENT MINIMUM $	MONTHLY PAYMENT GOAL $

• VISUAL TRACKER •

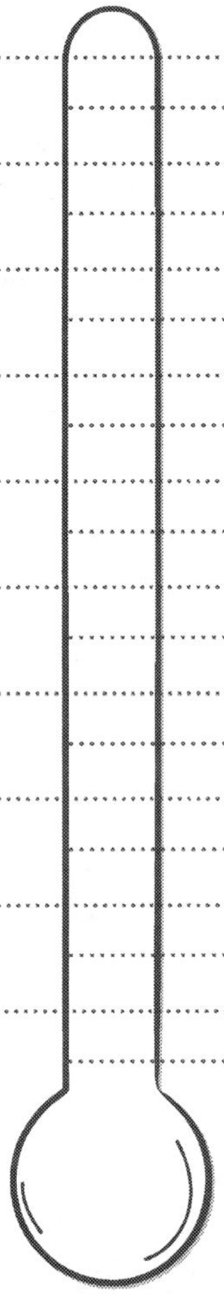

$ 100%

95%

$ 90%

85%

$ 80%

75%

$ 70%

65%

$ 60%

55%

$ 50%

45%

$ 40%

35%

$ 30%

25%

$ 20%

15%

$ 10%

5%

Color in the rows as you pay-off debt balance.

Notes

Debt Pay-off Tracker

DATE	PAYMENT	BALANCE
	$	$
	$	$
	$	$
	$	$
	$	$
	$	$
	$	$
	$	$
	$	$
	$	$
	$	$
	$	$
	$	$
	$	$
	$	$
	$	$

DATE	PAYMENT	BALANCE
	$	$
	$	$
	$	$
	$	$
	$	$
	$	$
	$	$
	$	$
	$	$
	$	$
	$	$
	$	$
	$	$
	$	$
	$	$
	$	$

Debt Pay-off Tracker

DEBT	CREDITOR
INTEREST RATE %	TERM
STARTING BALANCE $	PAYOFF DATE GOAL
MONTHLY PAYMENT MINIMUM $	MONTHLY PAYMENT GOAL $

• VISUAL TRACKER •

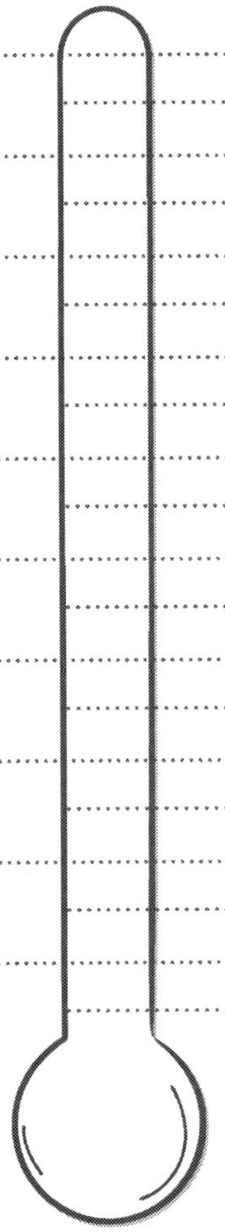

$ 100%

95%

$ 90%

85%

$ 80%

75%

$ 70%

65%

$ 60%

55%

$ 50%

45%

$ 40%

35%

$ 30%

25%

$ 20%

15%

$ 10%

5%

Color in the rows as you pay-off debt balance.

Notes

Debt Pay-off Tracker

DATE	PAYMENT	BALANCE	DATE	PAYMENT	BALANCE
	$	$		$	$
	$	$		$	$
	$	$		$	$
	$	$		$	$
	$	$		$	$
	$	$		$	$
	$	$		$	$
	$	$		$	$
	$	$		$	$
	$	$		$	$
	$	$		$	$
	$	$		$	$
	$	$		$	$
	$	$		$	$
	$	$		$	$
	$	$		$	$

Debt Pay-off Tracker

DEBT	CREDITOR
INTEREST RATE %	TERM
STARTING BALANCE $	PAYOFF DATE GOAL
MONTHLY PAYMENT MINIMUM $	MONTHLY PAYMENT GOAL $

• VISUAL TRACKER •

$ 100%

95%

$ 90%

85%

$ 80%

75%

$ 70%

65%

$ 60%

55%

$ 50%

45%

$ 40%

35%

$ 30%

25%

$ 20%

15%

$ 10%

5%

Color in the rows as you pay-off debt balance.

Notes

Debt Pay-off Tracker

DATE	PAYMENT	BALANCE	DATE	PAYMENT	BALANCE
	$	$		$	$
	$	$		$	$
	$	$		$	$
	$	$		$	$
	$	$		$	$
	$	$		$	$
	$	$		$	$
	$	$		$	$
	$	$		$	$
	$	$		$	$
	$	$		$	$
	$	$		$	$
	$	$		$	$
	$	$		$	$
	$	$		$	$
	$	$		$	$

Debt Pay-off Tracker

DEBT	CREDITOR
INTEREST RATE %	TERM
STARTING BALANCE $	PAYOFF DATE GOAL
MONTHLY PAYMENT MINIMUM $	MONTHLY PAYMENT GOAL $

• VISUAL TRACKER •

$ 100%

95%

$ 90%

85%

$ 80%

75%

$ 70%

65%

$ 60%

55%

$ 50%

45%

$ 40%

35%

$ 30%

25%

$ 20%

15%

$ 10%

5%

Color in the rows as you pay-off debt balance.

Notes

Debt Pay-off Tracker

DATE	PAYMENT	BALANCE	DATE	PAYMENT	BALANCE
	$	$		$	$
	$	$		$	$
	$	$		$	$
	$	$		$	$
	$	$		$	$
	$	$		$	$
	$	$		$	$
	$	$		$	$
	$	$		$	$
	$	$		$	$
	$	$		$	$
	$	$		$	$
	$	$		$	$
	$	$		$	$
	$	$		$	$
	$	$		$	$

Debt Pay-off Tracker

DEBT	CREDITOR
INTEREST RATE %	TERM
STARTING BALANCE $	PAYOFF DATE GOAL
MONTHLY PAYMENT MINIMUM $	MONTHLY PAYMENT GOAL $

• VISUAL TRACKER •

$ 100%

95%

$ 90%

85%

$ 80%

75%

$ 70%

65%

$ 60%

55%

$ 50%

45%

$ 40%

35%

$ 30%

25%

$ 20%

15%

$ 10%

5%

Color in the rows as you pay-off debt balance.

Notes

Debt Pay-off Tracker

DATE	PAYMENT	BALANCE
	$	$
	$	$
	$	$
	$	$
	$	$
	$	$
	$	$
	$	$
	$	$
	$	$
	$	$
	$	$
	$	$
	$	$
	$	$
	$	$

DATE	PAYMENT	BALANCE
	$	$
	$	$
	$	$
	$	$
	$	$
	$	$
	$	$
	$	$
	$	$
	$	$
	$	$
	$	$
	$	$
	$	$
	$	$
	$	$

DEBT PAY-OFF TRACKER

DEBT	CREDITOR
INTEREST RATE %	TERM
STARTING BALANCE $	PAYOFF DATE GOAL
MONTHLY PAYMENT MINIMUM $	MONTHLY PAYMENT GOAL $

• VISUAL TRACKER •

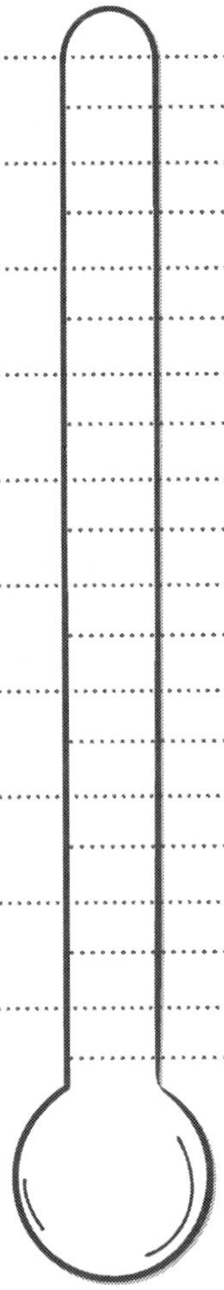

$ 100%

95%

$ 90%

85%

$ 80%

75%

$ 70%

65%

$ 60%

55%

$ 50%

45%

$ 40%

35%

$ 30%

25%

$ 20%

15%

$ 10%

5%

Color in the rows as you pay-off debt balance.

Notes

Debt Pay-off Tracker

DATE	PAYMENT	BALANCE	DATE	PAYMENT	BALANCE
	$	$		$	$
	$	$		$	$
	$	$		$	$
	$	$		$	$
	$	$		$	$
	$	$		$	$
	$	$		$	$
	$	$		$	$
	$	$		$	$
	$	$		$	$
	$	$		$	$
	$	$		$	$
	$	$		$	$
	$	$		$	$
	$	$		$	$
	$	$		$	$

DEBT PAY-OFF TRACKER

DEBT	CREDITOR
INTEREST RATE %	TERM
STARTING BALANCE $	PAYOFF DATE GOAL
MONTHLY PAYMENT MINIMUM $	MONTHLY PAYMENT GOAL $

• VISUAL TRACKER •

$		100%
	95%	
$		90%
	85%	
$		80%
	75%	
$		70%
	65%	
$		60%
	55%	
$		50%
	45%	
$		40%
	35%	
$		30%
	25%	
$		20%
	15%	
$		10%
	5%	

Color in the rows as you pay-off debt balance.

Notes

Debt Pay-off Tracker

DATE	PAYMENT	BALANCE	DATE	PAYMENT	BALANCE
	$	$		$	$
	$	$		$	$
	$	$		$	$
	$	$		$	$
	$	$		$	$
	$	$		$	$
	$	$		$	$
	$	$		$	$
	$	$		$	$
	$	$		$	$
	$	$		$	$
	$	$		$	$
	$	$		$	$
	$	$		$	$
	$	$		$	$
	$	$		$	$

DEBT PAY-OFF TRACKER

DEBT	CREDITOR
INTEREST RATE %	TERM
STARTING BALANCE $	PAYOFF DATE GOAL
MONTHLY PAYMENT MINIMUM $	MONTHLY PAYMENT GOAL $

• VISUAL TRACKER •

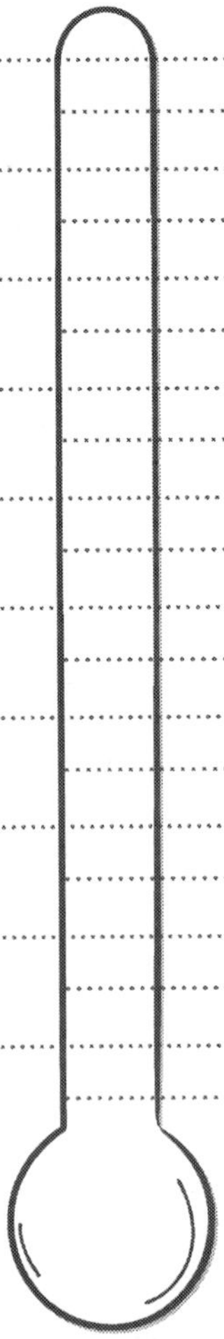

$		100%
	95%	
$		90%
	85%	
$		80%
	75%	
$		70%
	65%	
$		60%
	55%	
$		50%
	45%	
$		40%
	35%	
$		30%
	25%	
$		20%
	15%	
$		10%
	5%	

Color in the rows as you pay-off debt balance.

Notes

Debt Pay-off Tracker

DATE	PAYMENT	BALANCE	DATE	PAYMENT	BALANCE
	$	$		$	$
	$	$		$	$
	$	$		$	$
	$	$		$	$
	$	$		$	$
	$	$		$	$
	$	$		$	$
	$	$		$	$
	$	$		$	$
	$	$		$	$
	$	$		$	$
	$	$		$	$
	$	$		$	$
	$	$		$	$
	$	$		$	$
	$	$		$	$

Notes

Savings

PLAN AND MONITOR THE PROGRESS OF YOUR SAVINGS GOALS

Emergency Fund

• SAVINGS TRACKER •

Build an emergency fund to cover 6 months of expenses.

How to use this tracker- Each jar represents one month of expenses.
Each row represents ten percent of one month's expense.
Color in the rows as you save.

Savings Goal

$ ________ X 6 = $ ________

Monthly Expenses — Savings Goal

Value of Each Row

$ ________ ÷ 10 = $ ________

Monthly Expenses — Value of Each Row

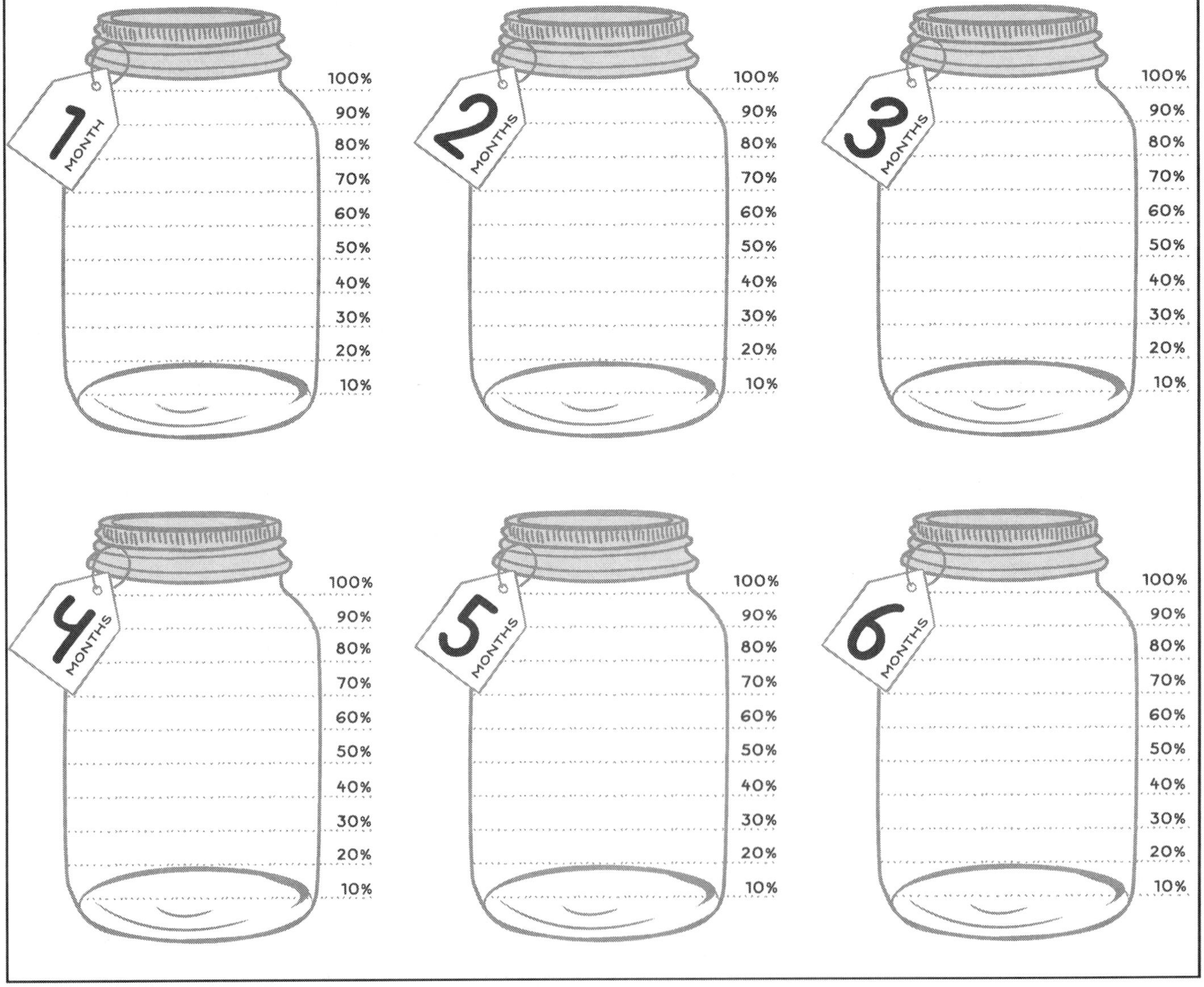

• SAVINGS TRACKER •

Emergency Fund

SAVINGS GOAL: $ ______________________

Date	Deposit	Date	Deposit
	$		$
	$		$
	$		$
	$		$
	$		$
	$		$
	$		$
	$		$
	$		$
	$		$
	$		$
	$		$
	$		$
	$		$
TOTAL SAVED	$	TOTAL SAVED	$

• SAVINGS TRACKER •

Fund For: ______________________

SAVINGS GOAL: $ ______________________

Date	Deposit
	$
	$
	$
	$
	$
	$
	$
	$
	$
	$
	$
	$
	$
TOTAL SAVED:	$

Notes:

____

____

____

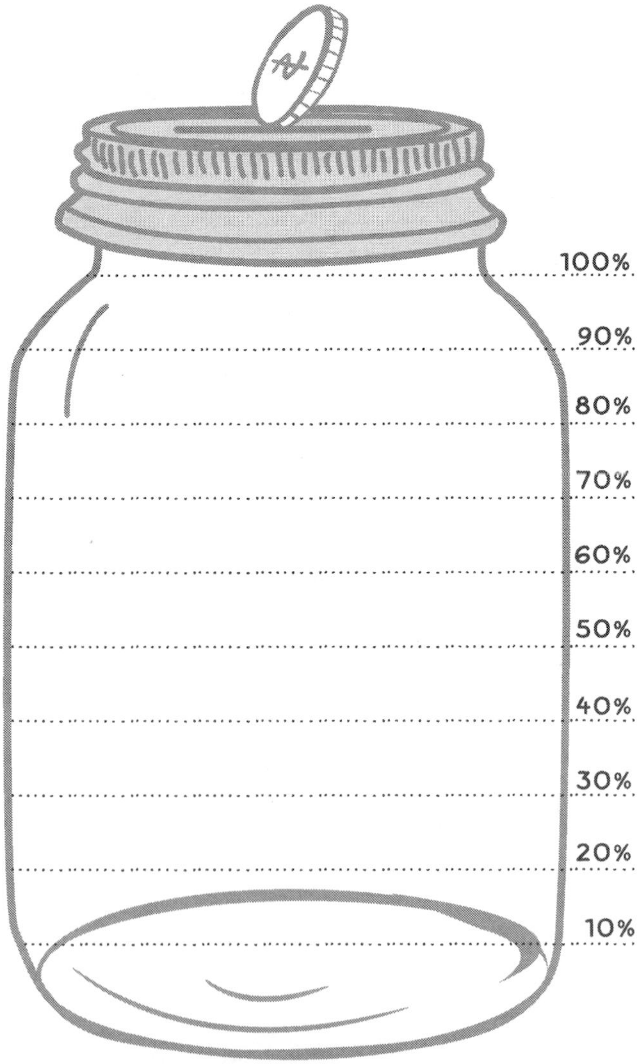

Color in the rows as you save.

• SAVINGS TRACKER •

Fund For: ______________________________

SAVINGS GOAL: $ ______________________

Date	Deposit
	$
	$
	$
	$
	$
	$
	$
	$
	$
	$
	$
	$
	$
TOTAL SAVED:	$

Notes: ______________________________

____

____

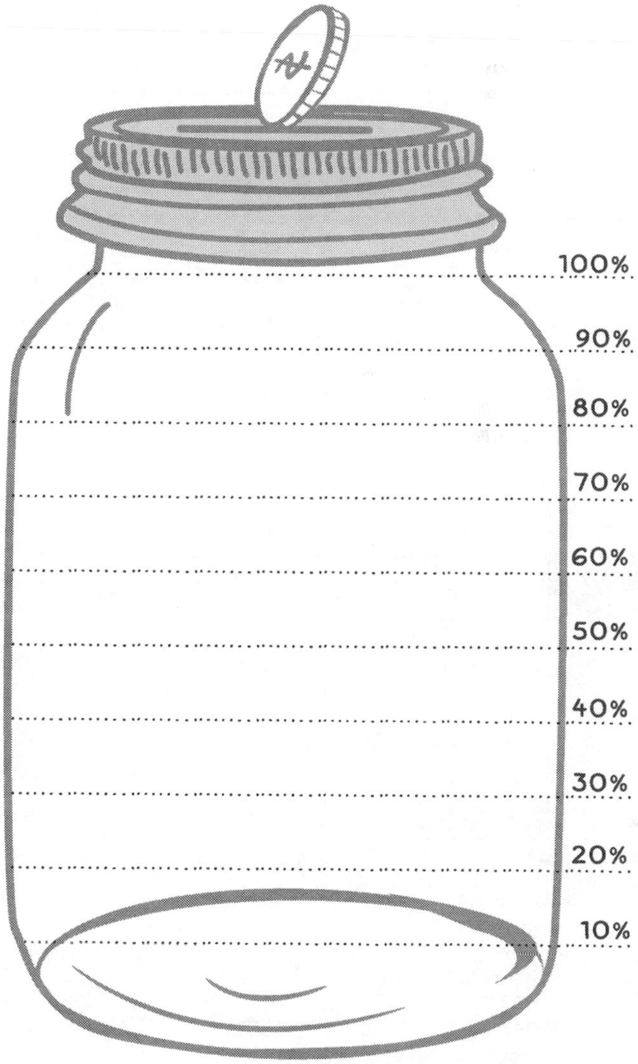

Color in the rows as you save.

• SAVINGS TRACKER •

Fund For: ______________________

SAVINGS GOAL: $ ______________________

Date	Deposit
	$
	$
	$
	$
	$
	$
	$
	$
	$
	$
	$
	$
	$
TOTAL SAVED:	$

Notes:

____

____

____

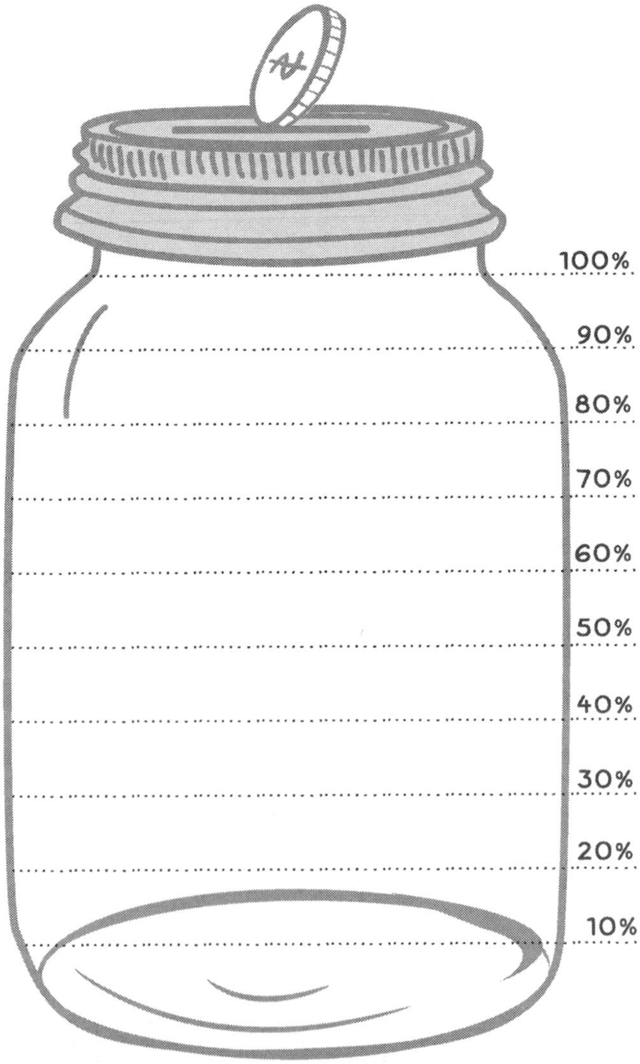

Color in the rows as you save.

• SAVINGS TRACKER •

Fund For: ______________________________

SAVINGS GOAL: $ ______________________

Date	Deposit
	$
	$
	$
	$
	$
	$
	$
	$
	$
	$
	$
	$
	$
TOTAL SAVED:	$

Notes: ______________________________

____

____

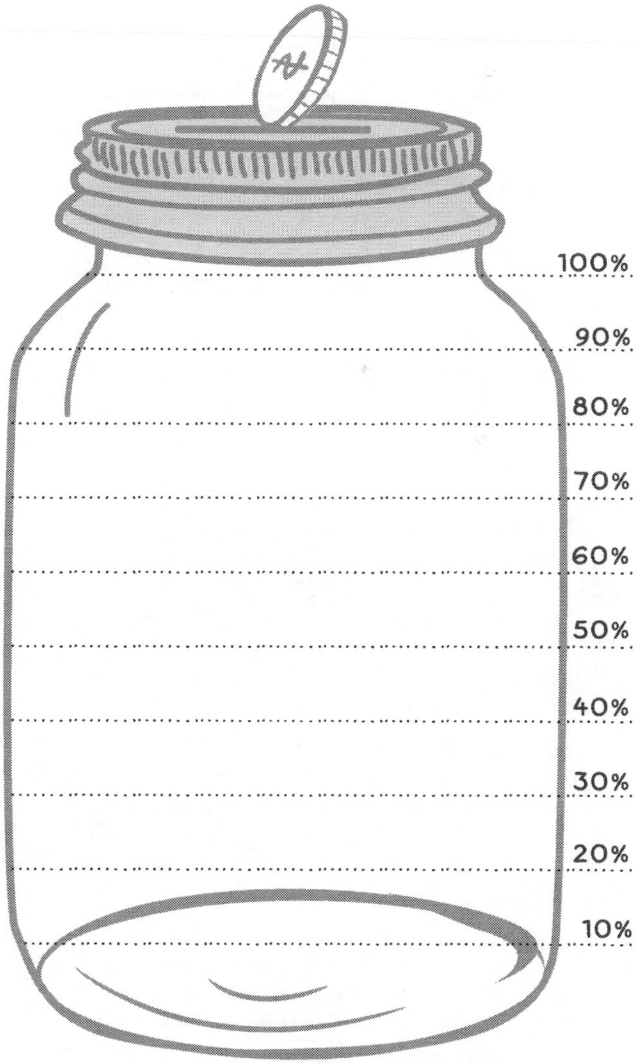

Color in the rows as you save.

• SAVINGS TRACKER •

Fund For: ______________________________

SAVINGS GOAL: $ ______________________

Date	Deposit
	$
	$
	$
	$
	$
	$
	$
	$
	$
	$
	$
	$
	$
TOTAL SAVED:	$

Notes:

____

____

____

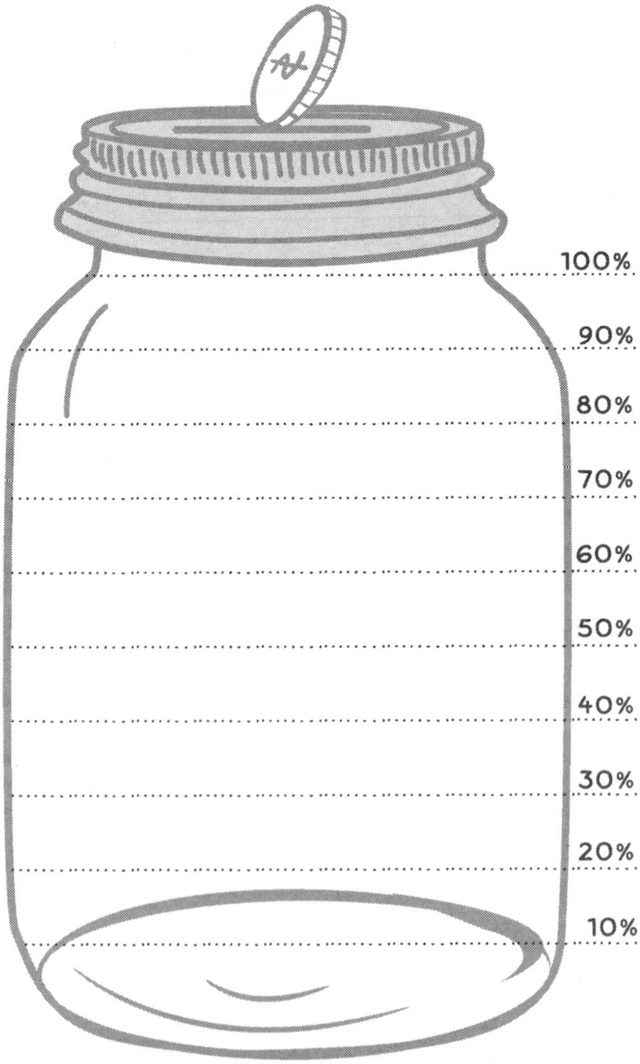

Color in the rows as you save.

• SAVINGS TRACKER •

Fund For: ______________________________

SAVINGS GOAL: $ ______________________

Date	Deposit
	$
	$
	$
	$
	$
	$
	$
	$
	$
	$
	$
	$
	$
TOTAL SAVED:	$

Notes: ______________________________

____

____

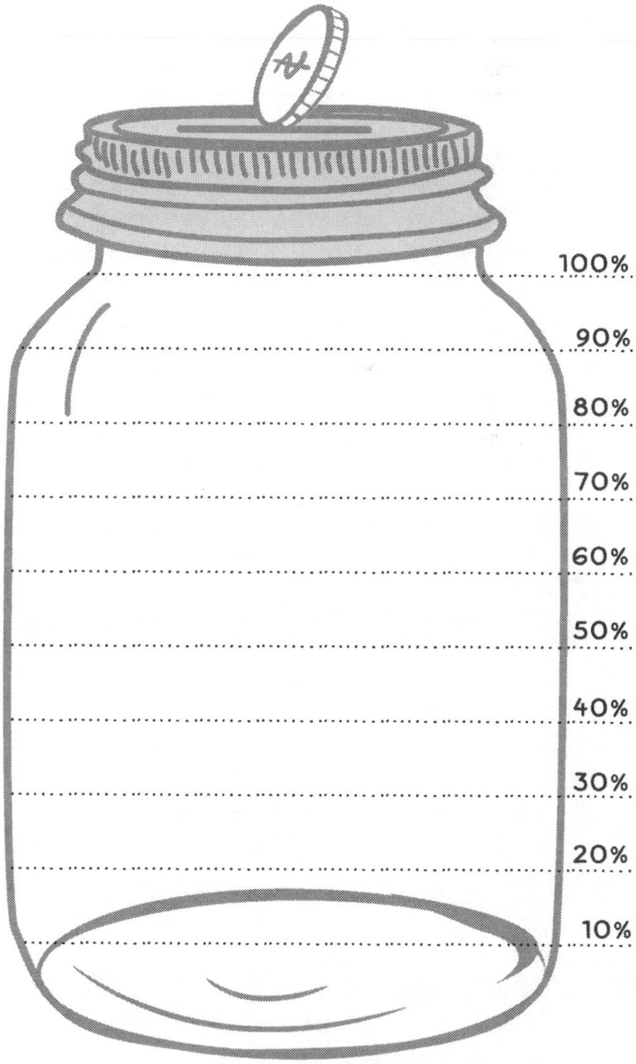

Color in the rows as you save.

• SAVINGS TRACKER •

Fund For: ______________________________

SAVINGS GOAL: $ ______________________

Date	Deposit
	$
	$
	$
	$
	$
	$
	$
	$
	$
	$
	$
	$
	$
TOTAL SAVED:	$

Notes:

____

____

____

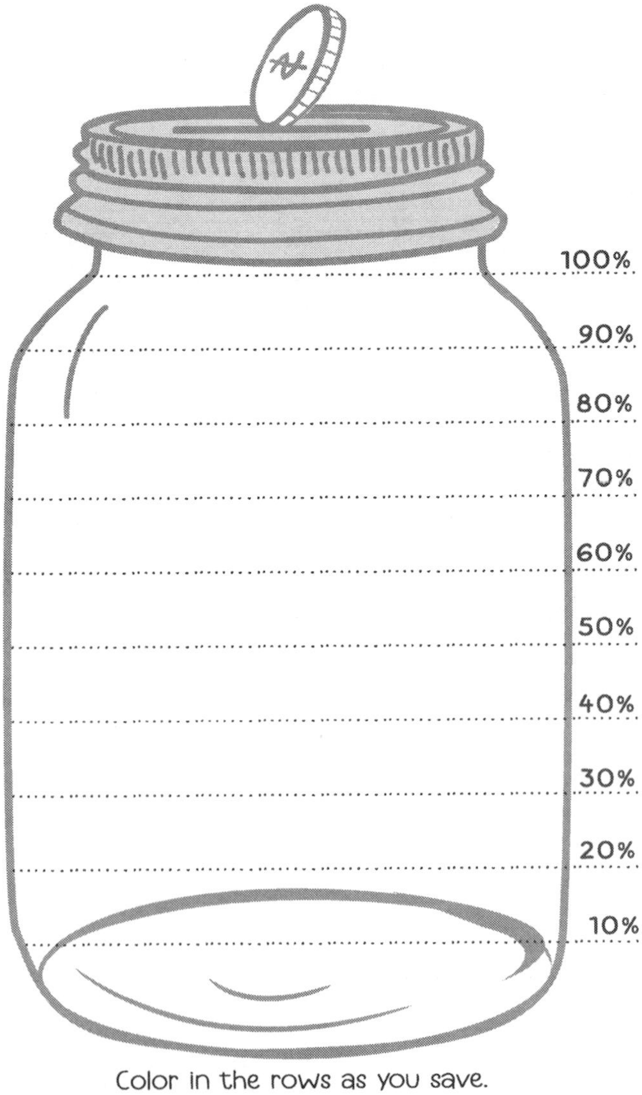

Color in the rows as you save.

• SAVINGS TRACKER •

Fund For: ______________________________

SAVINGS GOAL: $ ______________________

Date	Deposit
	$
	$
	$
	$
	$
	$
	$
	$
	$
	$
	$
	$
	$
TOTAL SAVED:	$

Notes: ______________________________

____

____

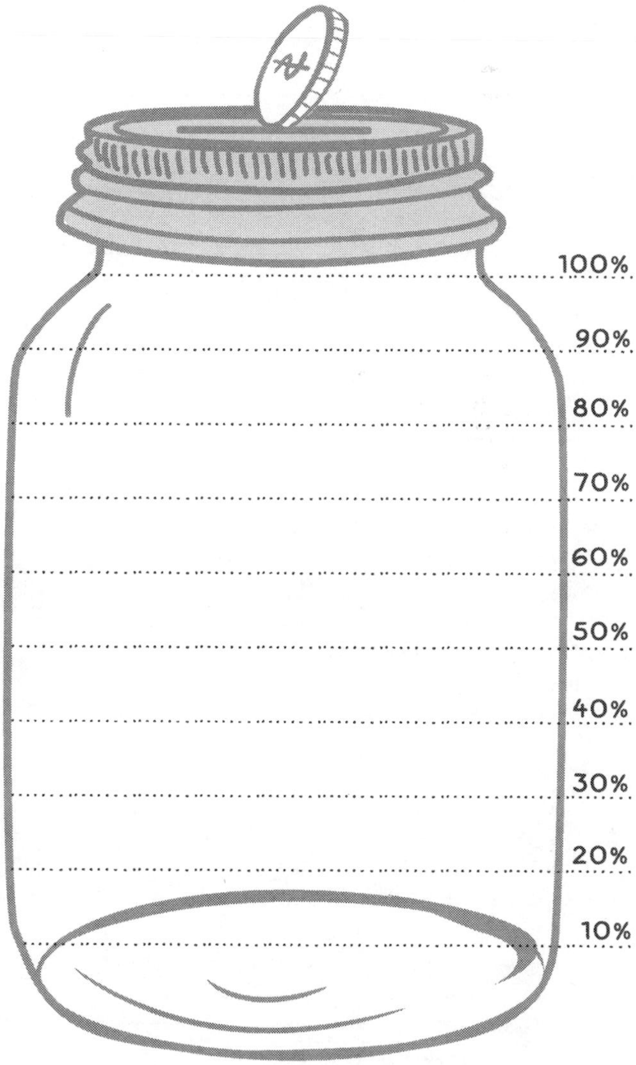

Color in the rows as you save.

• SAVINGS TRACKER •

Fund For: ______________________

SAVINGS GOAL: $ ______________________

Date	Deposit
	$
	$
	$
	$
	$
	$
	$
	$
	$
	$
	$
	$
	$
TOTAL SAVED:	$

Notes:

____

____

____

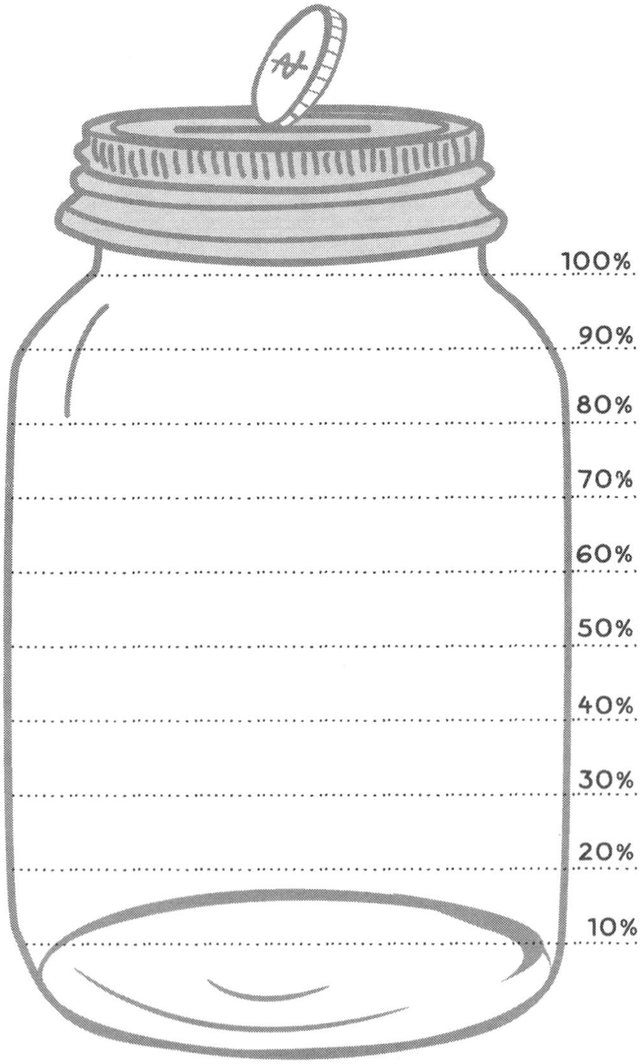

Color in the rows as you save.

• SAVINGS TRACKER •

Fund For: ______________________

SAVINGS GOAL: $ ______________________

Date	Deposit
	$
	$
	$
	$
	$
	$
	$
	$
	$
	$
	$
	$
	$
TOTAL SAVED:	$

Notes: ______________________

____

____

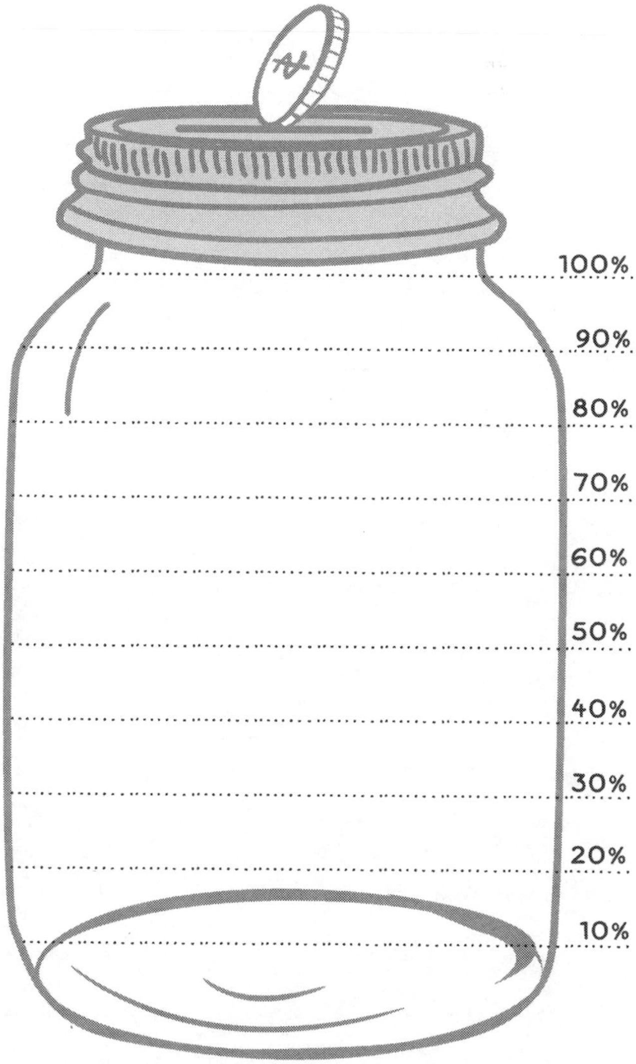

Color in the rows as you save.

Made in the USA
Monee, IL
08 November 2026

67377525R00063